IMAGES
of America

ST. LOUIS
OUT AND ABOUT IN THE GATEWAY CITY

The city's street-sprinkling wagons are proudly shown off in this parade along Market Street west from Twelfth Street. Taken around 1913, this photograph shows how brand-new equipment and a parade can create an event. Here, the parade not only attracted curious crowds, but also brought out photographers and journalists. (Courtesy of the Missouri Historical Society.)

ON THE COVER: This 1903 view looks west from Eighth Street to the Washington Avenue wholesale district as a team of horses clomp down the brick street pulling a delivery wagon. Several clothing and hat companies, along with shoe companies and milliners, were located in the buildings on this street. The wholesale district was booming at the time and was a good place to do business. (Courtesy of the Missouri Historical Society.)

IMAGES
of America

ST. LOUIS
OUT AND ABOUT IN THE GATEWAY CITY

Raymond Bial

ARCADIA
PUBLISHING

Published by Arcadia Publishing
Charleston, South Carolina

Printed in the United States of America

Library of Congress Control Number: 2019950047

For all general information, please contact Arcadia Publishing:
Telephone 843-853-2070
Fax 843-853-0044
E-mail sales@arcadiapublishing.com
For customer service and orders:
Toll-Free 1-888-313-2665

Visit us on the Internet at www.arcadiapublishing.com

St. Louis in 1832.

From an original Painting by Geo. Catlin in possession of the Mercantile Library Association.

This hand-tinted lithograph is based on a painting by the noted artist George Catlin. The fine work of art depicts a paddle wheel riverboat, aptly named the *St. Louis*, under steam on the Mississippi River in 1832. The St. Louis waterfront rises in the background. (Courtesy of the Library of Congress, Prints & Photographs Division.)

CONTENTS

ACKNOWLEDGMENTS

All uncredited images appear courtesy of the Missouri Historical Society, St. Louis. Others appear courtesy of the Library of Congress, Prints & Photographs Division, as indicated.

I especially appreciate the librarians, photograph researchers, and staff at the Missouri Historical Society and the Library of Congress for making their photography collections so readily available. This is very helpful to those of us who cannot get around as much as we did in our youth. The society and library are national treasures.

INTRODUCTION

St. Louis: Out and About in the Gateway City focuses on everyday life from the city's early days as a small trading post to its growth into a major metropolis. The book offers glimpses into the lives of common people and their daily activities, such as work and rest, ingenuity and relaxation, and responsibilities and amusements.

St. Louis has long been an epicenter of enterprise and ingenuity since explorers and settlers first passed through the trading post on the Mississippi River in the 1700s. When Pierre Laclède, a French fur trader, along with his assistant and stepson Auguste Chouteau, founded the city in 1764, it was already on its way to becoming a thriving frontier settlement. It was in an ideal location between the confluence of two powerful rivers, the Mississippi and Missouri (just north of St. Louis). There was also the Ohio River a few miles downriver. These were the "river roads" for explorers, traders, and settlers. From them, a young riverboat pilot adopted the name "Mark Twain."

Named after Louis IX, king of France, the city rapidly became a major port on the Mississippi River. Over the decades, the territory was claimed by Spain and France and then by a young, upstart nation born on the Fourth of July. Pres. Thomas Jefferson shrewdly acquired the territory from Napoleon Bonaparte in the deal of the century—the Louisiana Purchase of 1803. The city continued to grow through the first half of the 19th century as a river port. Shipping goods down to New Orleans and around the world, St. Louis became known as the "Gateway to the West" or "Gateway City" as it was the starting point for traders and settlers moving west overland or up the Missouri. In the US Census of 1870, St. Louis was already the fourth-largest city in the United States.

However, before that occurred, conflict over slavery and states' rights would lead to the Civil War, and St. Louis teetered on the sharp edge of this bloody fight. In the Missouri Compromise, the US Congress attempted to calm the regional, religious, and political debate when Missouri sought admission into the Union as a slave state in late 1819. The Fugitive Slave Act of 1850 only deepened the injustice of the Fugitive Slave Act of 1793. The US Supreme Court then ignited a firestorm with the Dred Scott case. This legal decision, arguably the worst in American history, led the nation into the Civil War. As a border state, Missouri had to take sides in the national conflict over slavery and regional differences.

Fortunately, the United States survived those four years of anguish and bloodshed, and St. Louis continued to flourish as a key port along the river. The city also came to be a robust manufacturing center and bustling metropolis. The strength, energy, and resiliency of the city and its people are amazing. By 1884, St. Louis had become its own unique blend of Southern charm and Northern industry—easy as New Orleans and intense as Chicago. The city had acquired its own distinct personality, like the Mississippi River with its calm surface that belies its powerful undercurrents.

This book carries the story forward from this point into the 20th century and shows how people shopped along brick streets, drove the first automobiles (often made in St. Louis), worked in one of the many popular breweries in the city, or enjoyed the beverages made in them. At one time, the city made everything from shoes to ships. *St. Louis: Out and About in the Gateway City* also looks at the entertainments of the day from downtown theaters to picnics in the park and popular hangouts. The book emphasizes how people literally got out and about along the Mississippi River and downtown streets in ever-changing vehicles—steamboats, wagons, carriages, streetcars, and automobiles. A man named Charles Lindbergh also got along just fine in a flimsy aircraft (by today's standards) called the *Spirit of St. Louis*.

The book touches upon hometown heroes, like Lindbergh, who embodied that spirit. It also looks at key events and crucial moments in the city's history: suffrage, racial relations, Depression, war, and Prohibition. It shows how people overcame or made sensible progress toward achieving a better life for everyone in St. Louis. Even in the worst of times, these photographs capture an easy laughter and love of life and depict activities ranging from ice skating and sledding in the depths of winter to swimming at a local pool in the hot summers. Our parents, grandparents, and great-grandparents knew how to be content and happy. They have clearly shown us the way to enjoy our lives, even in the face of adversity.

Most of their stories are told by these photographs, which are supplemented with captions. Several photographs provide fascinating insights about how "newsies"—some as young as four years old—sold local newspapers on the street. There is a picture of a 1901 electric car that was made not only in St. Louis but also well ahead of those by Edison and Ford. Another photograph shows Tennessee Williams's favorite theater. Also included is the poignant story of a young man named Walt Disney who had to sell his St. Louis–built 1928 Moon Roadster to help finance *Steamboat Willie* and introduce the world to a character named Mickey Mouse.

St. Louis has always been a city of energy and activity in which people like to get out and about. In this book, there is also a hint of whimsy in glancing over the past decades' styles of dress, social decorum, and amusements. Many images are flat-out funny—I got a kick out of these—and others are touching. There is nothing unnecessarily complicated about the city. Baseball legend Stan Musial epitomized the Gateway City in a single, plain sentence: "I have no hesitation to say that St. Louis is a great place in which to live and work."

St. Louis is known to be a sociable city, perhaps because it is composed of many neighborhoods. Even when standing stiffly for the camera, there are so many friendly faces in this book. I just loved the adventure of delving into past decades and looking into those faces. I hope that you enjoy looking at these photographs as much as I loved poring over thousands of images and looking into the lives of the men, women, and children who came before us.

One

FROM TRADING POST
TO RIVER CITY

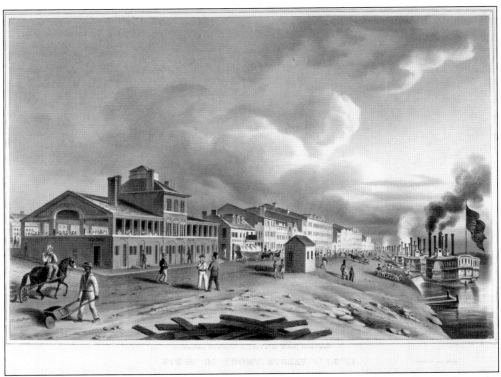

This hand-colored lithograph by J.C. Wild portrays a quaint view of Front Street along the levee from the southeast in 1840. At the time, the city was small yet bustling with river trade and growing by the day. The *Alton* is moored at the head of a long line of riverboats. Near this steamboat, two Natives Americans appear to be contemplating all the activity.

In this 1871 image of St. Louis from across the Mississippi River in East St. Louis, Illinois, A.R. Waud reveals a wide river crowded with steamboats and cargo along the shore. These were boom times for the port city and its river roads that linked adventurous and enterprising people throughout the nation.

THE LEVEE AT ST. LOUIS, MISSOURI.—Photographed by R. Benecke, St. Louis.—[See Page 957.]

Titled "The Levee at St. Louis, Missouri," this wood engraving, modeled after a photograph by Robert Benecke, was published in *Harper's Weekly* on October 14, 1871. The illustration depicts a romanticized view of the St. Louis riverfront, which was cluttered and hectic, but it shows a typical scene with steamboats moored on a levee bustling with horse traffic and men loading cargo.

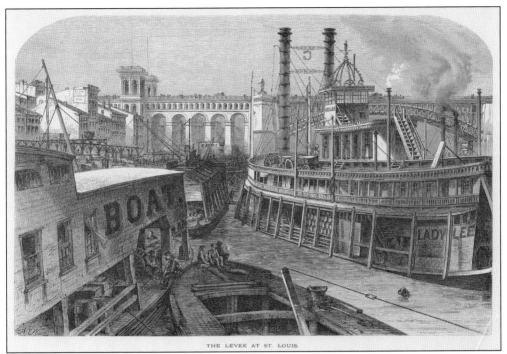

Titled "The Levee at St. Louis," this W. Roberts wood engraving, based on a photograph by A.R. Waud, was made in 1874. Originally published in *Picturesque America*, Vol. II, the illustration shows steamboats crowded together on the levee and dockworkers waiting for the next shipment.

The St. Louis levee is seen from the bridge looking south in this stereograph image from a photograph taken by Boehl and Koenig in 1879. The levee is covered with a variety of cargo along the shores and a row of steamboats into the distance.

Levee at St. Louis, Mo.

Taken in 1890, this photograph by Robert Benecke captures the hectic and often gritty atmosphere along the levee in St. Louis. Wagons are hauling loads of goods that need to be shipped, and drivers of empty wagons wait to be loaded with cargo from one of the many steamboats moored along the shore.

River Front. St. Louis, Mo.

This black-and-white postcard shows a view of the St. Louis riverfront around 1906. The steamboat *Spread Eagle* is passing alongside another steamboat docked at the landing. In the background, tall buildings rise up as the young city of St. Louis sprawls ever westward.

Photographed by Oscar Kuehn in 1910, these men are working among an assortment of barrels on the St. Louis levee. It appears that they are contemplating how many of the heavy barrels still need to be loaded and which barrels go on which steamboat.

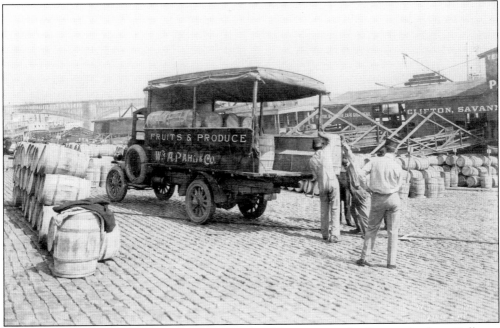

Enterprising people had to keep up with the times. Here, men are loading apples from Calhoun County, Illinois, onto a produce truck on the cobblestones of the St. Louis levee. The 1919 photograph by W.C. Persons shows how trucks steadily replaced horses and wagons as the preferred means of transporting goods on the river and throughout the city.

Passengers on an excursion cruise are leaving the steamer *St. Paul* and stepping onto the terra firma of the St. Louis levee around 1919. Everyone seems ready for an outing in the city. The women are dolled up in wide-brimmed hats and long dresses, and the men are wearing suits, as usual, along with the ubiquitous straw hats of the era.

In the twilight of a big city of bright lights, the steamer *President* is docked at the St. Louis levee. Taken by W.C. Persons from Eads Bridge about 1934, this photograph offers a striking view of a classic steamboat, along with the levee and city at night.

It was a quiet morning when this photograph was taken in May 1940, but the levee was quite busy as the city recovered from the Great Depression. Barges and riverboats, several with gangplanks down, line the riverfront at St. Louis. The Merchants Bridge can also be seen in the distance.

Sisters take a break from summer school at St. Louis University for an outing on the steamer SS *Admiral* on July 9, 1955. Taking in the sun on the Terrace Garden deck are, from left to right, Sisters M. Roberta of Ponca City, Oklahoma; Ann Cecile, Wichita, Kansas; M. Adella, Parsons, Kansas; M. Clarence, Parsons, Kansas; and M. Virginia, Wichita, Kansas.

Passengers lean on the railing to get a good look at the Mighty Mississippi and Eads Bridge from the lower deck of the steamer *Admiral*. The young lady at right is either shyly posing for the camera or at the age where she does not want to do anything with her family. It is not known who took this c. 1958 photograph.

This early view of Fourth Street looking south from Market Street was taken in 1866, just after the Civil War. The image is grainy, but offers a realistic view of a city recovering from war and embracing progress. Though they are horse-drawn, trolleys now rattle along tracks.

People stroll along a downtown street to do a little shopping, or perhaps they are on their way to work, around 1890. The tall buildings of a prosperous city now tower over them. Streetcars with electric cables strung overhead have already come to be the most convenient and sensible means of transportation in St. Louis. (Courtesy of the Library of Congress, Prints & Photographs Division.)

This photograph of horses and delivery wagons illustrates a traffic jam about 1900. The driver of a George Bosche Produce Company wagon is trying to pull away from the curb and work his way into the flow of traffic on Broadway near the corner of Cerre Street. However, no drivers will let him. Sound familiar?

It likely did not happen often, but one day around 1903, St. Louis went "hog wild." Pictured here is a large number of pigs trotting down the street at Thirteenth and Market Streets. It is not clear if the pigs were being driven to market or had broken loose. In either case, no one in the vicinity appears to be overly concerned.

At one time, there were plenty of horses and mules in St. Louis, but not many oxen. Here, in the late 1800s, a team of six oxen are pulling a wagon loaded with sacks of grain on a brick street.

This view of downtown St. Louis in 1903 shows Fourth Street looking north from a high perspective in the Planters' Hotel. The street is crowded with pushcarts, carriages, delivery wagons, and streetcars (also called trolleys or cable cars), which were becoming the principal means of transportation for most people. (Courtesy of the Library of Congress, Prints & Photographs Division.)

Olive Street, seen here looking west from Eighth Street, was dubbed the "Heart of Downtown St. Louis," at least according to photographer W.C. Persons, whose office was on the third floor of the building at left. The area was certainly abuzz in the 1920s, with people hoofing it, driving cars, and riding trolleys.

Looking north on South Broadway between Park Avenue and Barton Street, St. Louis appears quiet in the mist of a morning in the early 1900s. However, the area includes many thriving businesses, such as Lafayette Bank and Dr. C.D. Houston and Dr. K.W. Houston Dentistry. Once known as French Town, this area is one of the oldest business districts west of the Mississippi River.

This high view looking up Broadway north of Pine Street shows the rising skyline and the crowded streets of St. Louis in the 1910s. The streetcars appear to be overwhelmed as people try to get aboard to hurry home after a long day at work.

This view shows Broadway looking north from Locust Street in the early 1900s. This busy retail area had several popular stores, including Scruggs, Vandervoort & Barney department store; Mermod & Jaccard Jewelry Co.; Reid's Restaurant; Brandt's; Famous-Barr department store; and McClean's. This photograph was likely taken in the early morning when a lone streetcar and carriage were the only vehicles on the street.

This 1903 view looks west from Eighth Street to the Washington Avenue wholesale district as a team of horses clomp down the brick street pulling a delivery wagon. Several clothing and hat companies, as well as shoe companies, were located on this street. The wholesale district was booming at the time and was a good place to do business.

In this early 1900s view of Broadway, a variety of enterprises, including the Astor Theatre, line the left side of the street. Cars are parked on the curb and pedestrians stroll along the sidewalks or across the street as new contraptions called "automobiles" and a trolley roll down the street.

Around 1907, men and a newsboy pose in front of Walter J. Noble Whiskey and Wine at 1328 Market Street and Mielke's Lunch Stand at 1326 Market on the southeast corner of Market and Fourteenth Streets. There is a menu posted by the doorway of Mielke's. The Walter J. Noble window displays a variety of bottles and ads for various beverages, such as Pabst and Old Crow.

About 1909, a man strolls along the sidewalk of North Seventh Street, which is lined with busy enterprises. Signs advertise "Woman's Christian Cafeteria and Lunch Room," with "Supper Also Upstairs," along with safes and "Belts & Leather Novelties." A trolley and horse-drawn carriage can be seen in the background near a group of men repairing the brick street.

Between 1910 and 1915, a ragpicker ambles down the street with his horse and wagon at the intersection of Twelfth and Locust Streets. His wagon is piled high with mattresses to be recycled into other goods. People were frugal at the time. "Waste not, want not" was not simply a saying.

Taken around 1915, this photograph shows Twelfth Street looking north to Chestnut Street as a streetcar rumbles between rows of cars. People line the sidewalk under advertisements for Quaker Oats, Red Seal Dry Battery, St. Louis Taxicab Co's Public Garage, Assembly Buffet, Gold Medal Flour, Forshaw, Union Sample Case Co., Mulvihill, and Quick Meal.

This photograph was taken along Washington Avenue looking east toward Seventh Street around 1925. The double-decker Washington-Delmar bus is crowded with men sporting straw boaters and women in cloche hats. People crowd the street hoping to climb aboard for a jaunt around town.

The Grand National Bank at 505 North Grand Avenue is contending with a large crowd; the long line stretches far down the sidewalk past the Sugar Bowl and several theaters. This is believed to be a "bank run" after the stock market crash of October 1929. These runs continued until 1933 and only worsened the effects of the Depression.

Looking down Twelfth Street south to Market Street, this photograph captures the bright lights and triumphal arch honoring Thomas Edison and celebrating "Light's Golden Jubilee" on October 22, 1929. It is hard to imagine how recently electricity had come into people's lives at the time of this photograph, and how unimaginable it would be to live without it now.

On a rainy day on Washington Avenue looking east from Seventh Street is a convergence of old and new—a horse-drawn wagon and a streetcar rumbling up the street. It is about 1915. There is a soft mist in the air, and streets are glistening like patent leather.

A delivery wagon is parked on a brick-paved city street beside a wood-plank sidewalk. The location and date are unknown, but most likely, the wagon was parked downtown in the late 1800s, long before parking meters began to gobble up money along every curb. The wagon is open with only an umbrella over the driver's seat, which adds a nice touch. It was also useful on rainy days.

Two

VEHICLES

This Kinnell's horse snow shoes advertisement in the store window of Wiley Saddlery Company touts the worth of chain overshoes on hooves to keep one's horses from falling on the slippery streets. It was wintertime around 1900.

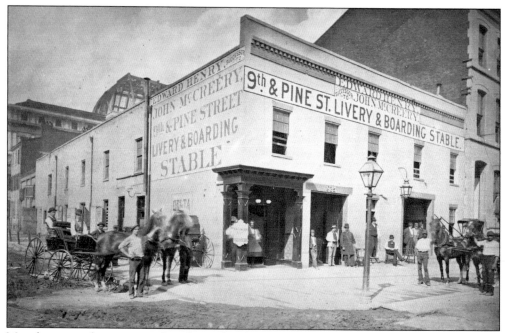

Men, horses, and carriages gathered outside Edward Henry's Ninth and Pine Streets Livery and Boarding Stable about 1884. A sign painted on the building reads that the livery was the successor to John McCreery. A saloon was also conveniently housed in the building.

In the early 1900s, a driver has backed his horse and wagon to the curb to more easily unload his delivery of coal to a saloon called the Blossom House. He is shoveling the coal down a chute into the basement next to the discreet "Ladies Entrance" to the drinking establishment.

Fred Lutz Jr.'s ice wagon is parked in the shade of a tree at 8417 Pennsylvania Avenue about 1908. Lutz was a dealer in ice during the summer and coal in the winter. It is more than likely that he was delivering ice on this hot summer day.

This advertising card by Compton and Company, printed around 1895, extols the virtues of Donk Brothers and Co.'s coal in various sizes and grades. The company's telephone number was "427."

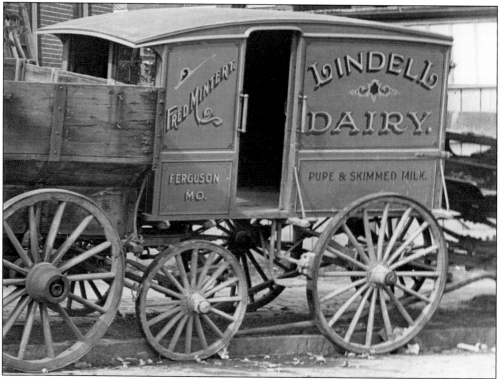

Taken by William G. Swekosky about 1920, this photograph shows a horse-drawn wagon of Lindell Dairy. The sides of the wagon advertise "Pure & Skim Milk," and the operator is identified as Fred Mintert from Ferguson, Missouri. Dairy wagons came by every morning to deliver milk, cream, and butter to the doorsteps of St. Louis homes.

In this undated photograph, two vehicles labeled "Anheuser-Busch Budweiser" appear to be tucked in among the steel supports of Eads Bridge. A stone arch can be seen in the distance, and streetcar tracks are in the foreground.

During the transition from horses to autos, Joseph A. Kutz sold supplies for both stables and garages at 3970 Chouteau Avenue. Among the products on offer were windshield curtains. While shopping, one could also grab a bite at "Wm S'mon's" Lunch Room, where a plate lunch cost 20¢ and regular dinner was 25¢.

A horse-drawn wagon and an early automobile are parked along the curb of a brick-paved street down by the river. It was the early 1900s, and every year, more autos with internal combustion engines came puttering along city streets.

Dressed for the occasion, two dignified couples are heading out on a Sunday drive in the country—to see and be seen—in their 1901 electric auto. Curiously, it is steered from the rear seat, lending credence to the term "backseat driver." Despite a few other quirks, this electric vehicle, built by A.B. Cull at the Briner Electric Company's shop, was way ahead of its time.

This group portrait shows four daring young men standing around and seated in a 1903 Pope-Toledo parked on the street outside A.L. Dyke Automobile Supply Company. Notes on the back identify the man standing at left as Robert F. Britton. A.L. Dyke is in the right rear seat.

Men gather near an automobile tire repair truck in front of H. Bender Firestone tire dealership at 4388 Olive Street in 1906. The business repaired all makes of tires. Automobile manufacturers, dealerships, and repair shops began to open in the city in the early 1900s. By 1908, St. Louis had issued 1,900 automobile licenses.

A variety of automobiles, along with a horse-drawn wagon from the St. Louis Bakery Company, are parked on the curb of an unidentified dirt street. A worker is leaning under the hood on one car and tinkering with the engine. It is an overcast day around 1910, and a row of brick buildings behind them advertise "Faust Beer" and "Restaurant."

Around 1914, a man waits patiently in his automobile, perhaps for that special someone. Will she ever be ready? He has come prepared with the top down, windshield up, and spare tire strapped to the side. The steering wheel is on the right side of the dashboard.

A group of women and men along with a baby stop in front of the Oscar Brackmann roadhouse with a sign for Anheuser-Busch Beer. They are motoring in three stylish vehicles and are dressed for the occasion. It was around 1914, and people were learning to appreciate the pleasure of taking a drive in the country.

Taken about 1915, this photograph shows a truck with an open-air bed, roof overhead, and rolled-up side curtains. With a hand-crank in the front, the truck was a practical vehicle for transporting cargo around the city. It is parked at an unidentified location with a wooden fence and a large advertisement for Richland Butter in the background.

In 1916, automobiles are being fueled up and serviced at one of the first gas stations in St. Louis, operated by the Pierce Oil Company at 4614 Washington Boulevard. Men are checking the oil and radiator fluid, as well as tire pressure, on an automobile behind the large "Drive Out" sign. A hose unravels across the street from a building to the car. The sign on top of the building reads, "Pennant Superior Quality Pierce Oil Corporation."

This 1929 Moon B-92 Windsor White Prince full sedan was manufactured by Moon Motors in St. Louis, named after carriage maker Joseph W. Moon, who established the company in 1905. Moon vehicles were popular as solid, mid-level cars, but the company had to close in 1930 during the Great Depression. Walt Disney reluctantly sold his beloved 1928 Moon Roadster to help finance *Steamboat Willie* and introduce Mickey Mouse to the world.

In 1900, streetcar employees went on strike for better hours, wages, and working conditions. During the strike, police forces were strained, and 2,500 citizens were deputized. These armed posse members are hanging around on cots in the United Railway carbarn during the streetcar strike. There to bust up the strike, they do not appear to be likable fellows.

These four men became deputies during the streetcar strike. Tony Faust is second from left; the others are unidentified. All carried rifles, and at least two packed sidearms too. These guys look somewhat ridiculous. During the strike, 14 people were tragically killed, and 200 were wounded in the bloody conflict.

Legs dangling over the sides, people sit packed on a long, open wagon at Fifteenth Street and Franklin Avenue during the streetcar strike from May 7 to the end of September 1900. The wagon became improvised transportation while the streetcars were shut down. The workers lost the strike, but the bitter conflict eventually led to reforms in St. Louis and throughout the state.

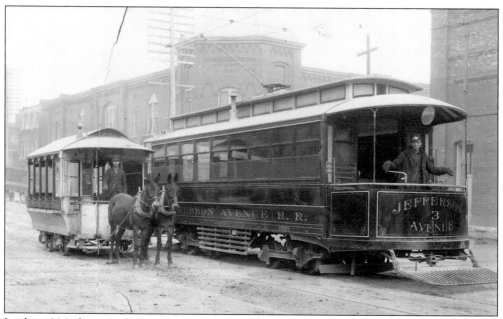

In this 1896 photograph, a streetcar on the Jefferson Avenue line and a smaller mule-drawn streetcar have pulled up next to each other. Before long, all the streetcars in the city would be powered by the amazing innovation called electricity.

In this early 1900s view looking west on Washington Avenue at Sixth Street, crowds have gathered on both sides of the street for an Elks parade. Many women have opened parasols against the glare from the summer sun as a long line of trolleys make their way down the street.

These dignified conductors pause with the Page Avenue streetcar just long enough to have their photograph taken for posterity. It is 1904, and they are at the street railway curve near the Skinker Road entrance to the Louisiana Purchase Exposition, also known as the St. Louis World's Fair.

This is a front view of Cass Avenue Streetcar No. 2343 at 5500 Belt Avenue and St. Louis Avenue in 1909. With an able and serious conductor at the controls, the streetcar is ready for action. A poster attached to the cowcatcher promotes the Charity Opera Festival in "Beautiful Delmar."

Rounding the corner on tracks laid on the brick streets, this streetcar is hard at work rattling along at South Tenth and Market Streets about 1915. It must have been a pleasant way to get around town.

This c. 1916 photograph shows the intersection of Washington Avenue and Broadway jammed with traffic. There were a couple of horse-drawn delivery wagons, but for the most part, streetcars and a steady stream of shiny new automobiles flow down the street or park at the curb.

This view shows Grand Avenue looking north from Olive Street in 1921. Cars line both sides of the street, and a streetcar has just stopped at a corner. Passengers are getting off, and others are climbing aboard. The Metropolitan Building at right is located at 508 North Grand Avenue.

Looking up Broadway north of Chestnut Street, this is a good view of a streetcar in action in September 1923. It is rolling down a street lined with cars while an automobile is headed in the other direction. With buildings rising on either side, the streetcar appears to be rolling through a deep canyon.

A double-decker, open-air bus and a streetcar have pulled up next to each other on Washington Avenue in the 1920s. They seem to be competing, and sadly, the less charming bus will soon prevail over the streetcar. For now, these men are all sharply dressed, and many have donned straw hats, which were the style of the day.

There is a lot of action at this intersection. Three streetcars negotiate the sharp corner at Vandeventer and Chouteau Avenues at 5:05 p.m. on August 4, 1925, as noted on the photograph, right in the midst of rush hour. One streetcar is taking on passengers while another offloads riders as automobiles slip past.

Opening the Fourteenth Street Viaduct on July 10, 1925, was cause for a celebration that brought out a crowd. The conductor stands behind the center window, and dignitaries gather behind him. The streetcar reads, "Bellefontaine," and features advertisements for Papendick Bakery Co. (Delicatessen Rye) and Anheuser-Busch soda (Grape Bouquet).

The Eads Bridge trolley station, at Third Street and Washington Avenue, is shown here as it appeared in 1925. Streetcars are lined up on the track, and a sign atop the station declares, "The Electric Way." After all, it was the "Era of Edison." Along with rumbling streetcars, autos, and trucks, pedestrians are busily going about their day.

Here is a broad view of the Eads Bridge trolley station in 1925. Along with streetcars on the track, there are automobiles rolling down the street and pedestrians ambling along the sidewalks. Note the double-decker bus.

People are lined up and waiting to climb aboard a streetcar that has properly stopped at the "Safety Zone" by the curb on the southwest corner of Washington Avenue and Seventh Street. It is around 1925, and people are also strolling down the sidewalk or lingering in front of storefronts.

Three

CHANGING WORLD

Francis Lance, who was five years old, sold newspapers regularly on Grand Avenue to earn a living. In May 1910, when he was photographed by Lewis Hine, the young newsie was regularly jumping on and off moving streetcars at the risk of life and limb. (Courtesy of the Library of Congress, Prints & Photographs Division.)

One of the many street children who survived by selling newspapers, making deliveries, and helping out on express wagons posed for this photograph. It was made by social activist Louis Hine on May 13, 1910. The young man is standing behind a wagon of the Adams Express Company in St. Louis. (Courtesy of the Library of Congress, Prints & Photographs Division.)

Harvey Nailing, a delivery boy for Kutterer Printing Company at 300 Olive Street, worked nine and a half hours a day. When he was photographed by Louis Hine in May 1910, he was standing with the pushcart that he used to make deliveries all over St. Louis. (Courtesy of the Library of Congress, Prints & Photographs Division.)

This diminutive newsie, nicknamed "Little Fattie," was just six years old. Despite his youth, the newspaperboy had already been on the job for a year when Lewis Hine took this photograph on May 9, 1910, in St. Louis. He might have had a tough life, but he sure was a cheerful little guy. (Courtesy of the Library of Congress, Prints & Photographs Division.)

Nicknamed "Livers" for some reason, this young newsie had a hard life. However, he also had bright eyes and a ready grin when he was photographed by Louis Hine in May 1910. Hopefully, he and all the other newsies in St. Louis went on to have well-paying jobs and happy lives. (Courtesy of the Library of Congress, Prints & Photographs Division.)

At 5:30 a.m. on Sunday, May 8, 1910, Lewis Hine photographed these boys as they were starting out into the streets with their newspapers from Burley's Branch at Twenty-third Street near Olive Street. All the boys look a little bleary-eyed, and they had a long day ahead of them. (Courtesy of the Library of Congress, Prints & Photographs Division.)

These newsies were selling newspapers on the streets and in saloons late into the night. In this photograph, taken by Lewis Hine at 9:00 p.m. on Saturday, May 7, 1910, the newspaperboys were still at work with papers in hand. One wonders when (or what) they ate and where they slept at night. (Courtesy of the Library of Congress, Prints & Photographs Division.)

This young truant was selling newspapers at Broadway and Locust Streets at 11:00 a.m. when he was supposed to be studying in school. When he was photographed by Lewis Hine in May 1910, he appeared to be happy with his job on the street. One wonders what he made of his life. (Courtesy of the Library of Congress, Prints & Photographs Division.)

Dedicated to a worthy cause, these women gathered for a board meeting in 1912 at the first headquarters of the Equal Suffrage League of St. Louis. They sought full voting rights for women, and they meant business. They were persistent, and they prevailed nine years later.

In a fiery speech, Kate Richards O'Hare addresses a crowd in front of the St. Louis Courthouse on National Women's Suffrage Day, May 2, 1914. She was an activist, editor, and orator. O'Hare became nationally known for her unjust prosecution and imprisonment during World War I.

An unidentified speaker in a top hat politely addresses a large crowd gathered on the steps of the St. Louis Courthouse on National Women's Suffrage Day, May 2, 1914. By the looks of it, the man has been making a convincing argument in favor of voting rights for women.

In 1916, these members of the St. Louis Equal Suffrage League embarked on a journey across the state to promote women's suffrage. Three years later, on July 3, 1919, Missouri women gained voting rights when the state became the 11th in the nation to ratify the Suffrage Amendment (later named the 19th Amendment) to the US Constitution.

These young women in light dresses are twirling their parasols in the Preparedness Parade of June 3, 1916. The parade was meant to "give expression to the general demand for adequate armed defenses," according to the *St. Louis Republic*. Gov. Elliot W. Major and Mayor Henry Kiel observed the four-hour event from a reviewing stand in front of the St. Louis Club.

Perhaps it is true—there is something about a man in uniform. These two young women have draped themselves around a soldier who does not seem to mind at all. The young women are outfitted in sporty, knee-length dresses in the style of 1917–1918. The soldier is most likely on leave after training before he goes "over there" to the battlefields of Europe.

Six young African Americans gather around a cardboard cutout of a soldier advertising Liberty Bonds at the corner of Jefferson and Market Streets in 1918. One young man is saluting the photographer. A note accompanying the print reads, "No 126 4th Liberty Loan sign with last part of first draft of Negroes on it. Picture taken on the North East Corner of Jefferson an market. Sept 25 1918."

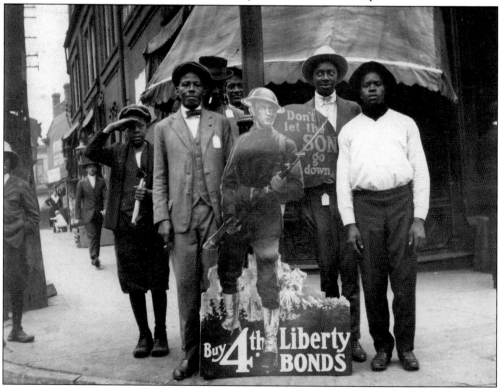

This sign urges patriotic Americans to purchase Liberty Bonds. Posted at the southeast corner of Jefferson and Market Streets, the sign is adorned with two American flags at the corners. A handwritten note in the margin dates the photograph to September 25, 1918.

These young ladies are celebrating Armistice Day with horns and noisemakers. The women wear banners and wild hats. They are standing in front of a house and holding or blowing on paper horns. Some also wave small flags, and one is holding what appears to be a homemade loudspeaker. A handwritten note provides the time and date, November 11, 1918, at 1:15 p.m.

The ladies of St. Louis warmly welcomed home soldiers from the 314th Engineers during a stop in St. Louis. Here, a woman holds the hands of two soldiers as they and their pals hang out of the windows of their train car. A description by R.J. Walker on the back of the photograph reads, "Saying hello on return of the 314th Engrs at St. Louis."

St. Louis was once thick with breweries—at one time, there were 108, which is quite a few. Chris Staehlin's Phoenix Brewery opened in 1864 and closed two years later. Like so many other breweries, it had a short life. Here, workers stare back at the camera, and many raise mugs of beer to the health of the photographer.

Around 1870, this group of sharply dressed men hoist glasses of beer and pose with a Lafayette Brewery keg. They appear to be proud of their product. Lafayette Brewery opened in 1864 and closed in 1874. Located at 1820 Cass Avenue and Nineteenth Street, it was owned by T. Brinkwirth and Frank Griesedieck.

The burly workers of the Anheuser-Busch Brewery, many with mugs of frothy beer in hand, posed for this photograph in 1891. They are gathered on steps (presumably at the brewery) with three kegs of beer front and center.

THE LADIES HOME JOURNAL

Endorses
Beer as Opposed to Patent Medicines.
Of course, a pure, wholesome beer
is meant—that is

Budweiser

Mr. Edward Bok, editor of The Ladies' Home
Journal, in a page article in the May issue gives a
list of 36 medicines, with official analysis, asserting
them to contain **12 to 47 per cent. of Alcohol!**

And he adds in black type:
"In connection with this list, think of beer, which
contains only from two to five per cent. of
alcohol, while some of these 'bitters' contain
ten times as much, making them stronger than
whisky, far stronger than sherry or port, with
claret and champagne way behind."

Mr. Bok continues:
"A mother who would hold up her hands in holy
horror at the thought of her child drinking a glass
of beer, which contains from two to five per cent. of
alcohol, gives to that child with her own hands a
patent medicine that contains from seventeen to
forty-four per cent. of alcohol."

Budweiser contains only 3 ⁸⁄₁₀ per cent. of
alcohol. It is better than pure water because
of the nourishing qualities of malt and the
tonic properties of hops.

Budweiser is pre-eminently a family beverage;
its use promotes the cause of true temperance
—it guards the safety of health and home.
Budweiser is

"King of Bottled Beers"
Bottled only at the home plant of the
Anheuser=Busch Brewing Ass'n, St. Louis, U.S.A.

FOR MAY 1904

This ad touts a 1904 article in *Ladies Home Journal* that endorses beer as superior to patent medicines. It states, "Of course, a pure, wholesome beer is meant—that is Budweiser." The ad claims that "Budweiser is pre-eminently a family beverage; its use promotes the cause of true temperance—it guards the safety of health and home."

Three men have sidled up to the bar in the Magnolia Saloon about 1900. They are enjoying a drink or two after work. Two very professional-looking bartenders stand at attention ready to pour each of their customers another glass of beer or shot of their favorite whiskey before they head home for dinner.

Young and old alike gather in front of the Thomas H. Schuetz Exchange Saloon in the early 1900s to formally pose for this group portrait. At least one man is enjoying a sip of beer, which was a popular beverage among the many German immigrants. The boys and girl are probably there to take their fathers home.

The sign below the storefront windows for Fellhauer Brothers (August and Martin) claims that the enterprise sells fine whiskies at wholesale prices along with tobacco and cigars. There is an impressive display of bottles in the window. In 1907, the business was located at 3315 Olive Street, just west of Leonard Avenue.

Outside in fair weather was a pleasant way to enjoy a beer or two, and beer gardens were once very popular in St. Louis. Everyone appears to be having a very good time at Louis Weider's Beer and Wine Garden when this photograph was taken by Richard Gruss about 1910. This trendy establishment was located at 700 South Broadway.

A young woman scowls beneath a sign forbidding the use of intoxicating liquor, tobacco, profanity, and vulgarity. The c. 1905 photograph was taken in a small town on the outskirts of St. Louis.

Police officers from the Carr Street station look on wistfully as they supervise the draining of a mash vat at an illicit distillery on Franklin Avenue. This photograph of whiskey mash flowing into storm sewers was taken in the early 1920s after Prohibition had become the law of the land.

Three members of the Busch family—(from left to right) Adolphus Busch III, August Busch Sr., and August Busch Jr.—pose with the first case of post-Prohibition beer. The case of Anheuser-Busch beer was sent to Pres. Franklin Delano Roosevelt. August Busch Sr. holds an envelope addressed to the White House.

Bartender Alex Piantanida and an unidentified barmaid serve a couple at the Old Rock House Saloon in the 1930s. The Old Rock House was one of the oldest buildings in the city and later became a tavern and music venue. It was to be restored as a historic site but was never rebuilt.

On May 10–11, 1927, Charles Lindbergh tested the *Spirit of St. Louis* by flying from San Diego to New York City, with an overnight stop in St. Louis. Young, calm, and confident, Lindbergh stands beside his plane at Lambert Field. He arrived in New York after 20 hours and 21 minutes, which was a transcontinental record.

A beaming Lindbergh poses at Lambert Field after his return to St. Louis from his historic New York–to–Paris flight on June 8, 1927. Harold K. Bixby, who supported the venture and suggested the name *Spirit of St. Louis* for the airplane, is looking over the courageous young pilot's shoulder at left.

It seems that everyone in the city came out for this ticker tape parade in downtown St. Louis for Charles Lindbergh on June 18, 1927. It was the second day of a three-day reception in honor of the daring young flier. No one, including Lindbergh, anticipated such a warm homecoming.

Lindbergh's parade on June 18, 1927, eases along Olive Street past Eighth Street, as he and Mayor Victor Miller ride westbound in a flower-decked car. People crowd the sidewalks. Lindbergh, his airplane, and his daunting flight truly represented the "spirit of St. Louis."

A huge crowd blankets much of Art Hill in Forest Park to greet Lindbergh as he flies over them in the *Spirit of St. Louis*. It is June 19, 1927, and seemingly overnight, the young aviator had become the hero of just about everyone in St. Louis. The flyover was Lindbergh's way of thanking everyone in the city.

Four

GOING TO BUSINESS

Taken around 1900, this photograph shows a brick building with a horse-drawn buggy parked against the sidewalk. A woman leans out the second-floor window. The front street-level window advertises Mike Johnson's boot and shoe repair, with some very reasonable prices.

In the early 1900s, things were hopping downtown. People could choose to get a shoeshine for a nickel or shoes dyed for a quarter. A streetcar rumbles past, and a delivery wagon is pulling into sight. But most enticing is Milford's Oyster House and Restaurant at 209 North Sixth Street, where one could feast on the most delectable of seafoods.

Around 1906, several pedestrians amble along the sidewalk in front of New Lindell Hotel and Fellhauer wine shop at 705–707 Sixth Street. No one seems to be in a hurry. This photograph, attributed to Charles Clement Holt, captures a moment in the everyday life of St. Louis.

Carl Panick, a customer in search of supplies, visits with Emil G. Decker, the owner of Decker Hardware Store, at 3330 South Broadway in the 1920s. The two men stand across the counter from each other surrounded by shelves and counters crammed with tools and hardware. No one could say it was not a well-stocked store.

Here is a night view of Grand Avenue around 1930, with a brightly lit neon sign for Sugar Bowl candies and Sunfreze ice cream. It was the perfect spot for anyone who had a sweet tooth and wanted a treat after a show at the Missouri Theater (in the distance) or other theater on the street.

This nighttime photograph of the Famous Cleaning and Dyeing Company's storefront with the door open was taken in 1934. Employees and customers are standing behind and around the counters inside. This shop cleaned and blocked hats, sponged and pressed suits, dyed shoes, and cleaned dresses—while patrons waited—so that everyone could dress in style.

This 1934 photograph shows the interior of Famous Cleaning and Dyeing Company. Standing behind the counter and along the wall, clerks are ready to wait on customers. Several hats are displayed on the front counter, and a woman is browsing the selection of merchandise on the opposite counter and shelves.

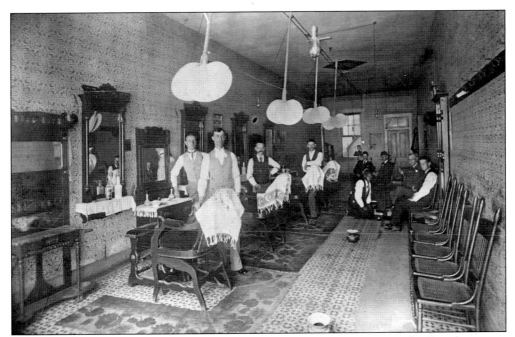

The interior of this unidentified barbershop shows barbers, customers, and a shoeshine man sometime between 1890 and 1899. With a row of chairs and four barbers on duty, there likely were not long waits at this shop. One could always get a shoeshine, which sadly was one of the few jobs available to African Americans.

About 1900, these men gather in front of the Globe Shaving Parlor at 1015 Carr Street. A horse is hitched and waiting while the men pose. The group includes a police officer, two men sporting white jackets, and others wearing coats and bowler hats. The familiar striped pole clearly identifies the enterprise as a barbershop.

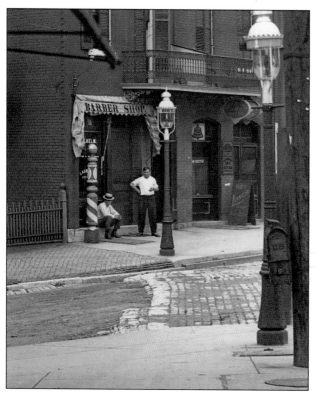

In this c. 1910 photograph attributed to Charles Clement Holt, two men are visiting outside of Andrew Wilhelm's barbershop at 3687 South Broadway at the corner of Miami Street. Conveniently located next door, John J. Roettig's saloon advertises American ABC Beers and a hot lunch.

In 1917, men and children gather on a corner while a boy nonchalantly leans against the doorframe of an unidentified barbershop. It seems to be an ideal place to swap stories and share a little gossip.

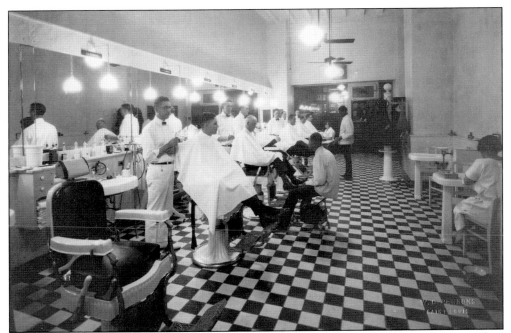

In this 1920s photograph by W.C. Persons, customers in white capes occupy a row of chairs while barbers clip hair. African American men polish shoes, and a manicurist waits for her next customer in this spiffy barbershop (possibly City Club). At the time, African Americans were typically limited to menial jobs.

The proprietor (at left) and a seated customer with a cane are lounging in A. Moll groceries around 1895. Despite the casual atmosphere, the proprietor is dressed to the nines in suit and tie. The store offers a wide variety and abundance of vegetables and fruits. The shelves are also crammed with canned foods and dry goods, such as coffee, tea, sugar, and flour. (Courtesy of the Library of Congress, Prints & Photographs Division.)

This photograph captures the A. Moll Grocer Company at 5659 Delmar Boulevard north of DeBaliviere Avenue as it appeared in 1932. A sign on the roof declares, "Moll's: St. Louis' Most Complete Food Market." A clock is featured at the front of the store along with reminders that A. Moll was established in 1858. Attractive displays can be seen through the windows.

A boy and some men stand on the brick sidewalk in front of an unidentified grocery in the late 19th century. There are displays of fresh produce, including bananas, in front of the store window. A woman is also sitting on the roof, perhaps so that she can literally "get in the picture."

In this photograph from 1904, horse-drawn delivery wagons jam the Third Street Market as boys and men jostle for space and try to find the best location to set up their wagons and stands. Most are open-air wagons carrying fruits and vegetables. Pulled by a pair of white horses, the wagon in front is loaded with watermelons.

Farmers' markets are hardly a new concept in St. Louis or elsewhere in the country. This is how the stalls and vendors at Soulard Market appeared on a busy morning in 1910. Shoppers wandered around the crowded street looking for bargains in fresh vegetables, fruit, and merchandise.

About 1910, children line up for after-school confections outside F. Hochman Grocer at 7800 Michigan Street (on the corner of Courtois Street). On the two-story brick store, the proprietor has posted signs that advertise Eagle Stamps and "Staple & Fancy Groceries."

This wagon traffic on Commission Row in the 700 block of Third Street illustrates how crowded the wholesale district was in the early morning. The c. 1910 photograph, taken by Charles Clement Holt, shows that wagons were still the preferred vehicle for making deliveries in St. Louis.

About 1910–1919, Commission Row (also known as Produce Row) was a busy wholesale market with young men unloading and displaying wooden crates and bushel baskets heaped with fresh produce at bargain prices. Ralph L. Jones Restaurant was also conveniently located along the row.

Around 1915, these shoppers, young and old alike, gathered by the crates of fresh vegetables and fruits offered for sale on the sidewalk in front of the Theodore Prieshoff Grocery. The grocery store was located at 1929 East Grand Avenue, near the North Grand water tower. It is a sunny day, and it is good to be outside.

This photograph shows the Thomas Rizzo produce stand and its courteous and knowledgeable employees at 123 Union Market as it appeared in 1919. Dressed in white shirts and aprons, the clerks, probably family members, are ready to help customers select the freshest fruit and vegetables.

This is how the meat counter at a grocery store, possibly Lindwedel Grocery at 2801 Missouri Street, looked when photographed by Richard Gruss around 1928. The store is well stocked with sides of beef, whole hogs, and other delectable cuts, along with five butchers in white coats ready to cut perfect steaks and chops.

Around 1930, a woman and young girl, likely her daughter, have stopped at a roadside stand to look over the baskets of fresh potatoes, onions, and other vegetables, along with peaches, blueberries, and other fruit. Perhaps they also picked up a couple dozen eggs, tomatoes, and some homemade preserves.

This old photograph of the interior of the Pewinski grocery store shows canned and boxed goods piled on shelves and counters. In the background are two men and two women, most likely the proprietors and clerks. A note on the photograph reads, "About 1942. South East Corner 13th and Madison St. L. Mo."

This woman is proudly stocking and displaying heads of iceberg lettuce at Soulard Market in 1971. She has reason to be pleased with the produce she can offer to her customers. She has grown and carefully tended the lettuce, peaches, green beans, and other vegetables and fruit on her own farm.

In this 1940s photograph of an unidentified grocery store, canned goods and ketchup bottles are stacked in the window. A sandwich-board sign out front reminds pedestrians that a "Merchants Lunch" can also be had there.

Five

ROARING TWENTIES, GREAT DEPRESSION, AND WAR

Glowing in the bright lights of 1925, the Rivoli Theater at Sixth Street south of Olive Street was showing *The Mad Whirl*, starring May McAvoy. Built in 1896 as Caesar's Café, the restaurant was redesigned into a theater by Charles Ramsey, an associate of Louis Sullivan. The stunning theater became a St. Louis city landmark, but was razed in 1983.

When W.C. Persons photographed the Washington Theater and Skydome around 1925, it was featuring the "all talkie" *Speakeasy* movie, along with Movietone News. Alex Shoe Store was next door, with several other retailers along the street.

Here is the old entrance to the New Grand Central Theater at 702 North Grand Boulevard as it appeared in 1925 with United Cigar Stores Co. conveniently located next door. The theater opened in 1913 and featured vaudeville, silent movies, and early talkies. The marquee announced that *Her Night of Romance* was showing. Another sign reads, "30 Jazz Hounds will do their stuff in the New Grand Central Jazz Derby, starting April 11."

This atmospheric photograph offers a bird's-eye view looking west on Market Street late at night. The street is brightly lit with glistening pavement and deep shadows reminiscent of film noir of the era. This photograph was taken by Richard Moore in the 1930s.

Workers are carefully making floral arrangements backstage at the Fox Theatre around 1929. Taken by W.C. Persons, the photograph shows how theaters were not only elegant, even palatial, but also adorned with bouquets of fresh flowers and other extra touches.

A young woman is playing the Wurlitzer organ at the Fox Theatre in 1929. The photograph by W.C. Persons also shows the elaborate curtain and trim around the organ. Going to the movies was once an event. Before talkies became all the rage, musical accompaniment lent a feeling of suspense, drama, and humor to the silent movies of that era.

In 1929, the Fox Theatre marquee and facade were brightly lit and decorated to celebrate the movie house during its silver jubilee. In the 1920s, St. Louis had more theaters per capita than any other American city, including New York. Located at 527–529 North Grand Avenue, the Fox was one of them.

In July 1930, a crowd waits patiently on the pavement for the next movie at the St. Louis Theatre. "Baby Rose Marie in Person" and *Inside the Lines*, starring Betty Compton, are advertised on the marquee. The theater also touts that it was the "Coolest Spot in Town."

On this hot summer day in 1930, the St. Louis Theatre is showing *Lawful Larceny* with signs declaring it is "cool inside," "cooled by refrigeration," and "the coolest spot in town." Pedestrians and a legion of ushers congregate outside the box office and a steam locomotive for promotion.

In the 1930s, a truck slowly makes its way down the street in a national relief parade during the Great Depression. The vehicle and riders are promoting the worth and contributions of theaters. St. Louis theaters enriched the city not only culturally, but also economically.

Around 1937, the West End Lyric Theater was showing *Fifty Roads to Town*, starring Don Ameche and Ann Sothern, and *Call It a Day*, starring Olivia de Havilland and Ian Hunter. When playwright Tennessee Williams lived in St. Louis as a teenager, he preferred this first-run movie house over others. The theater was located at 4819 Delmar Boulevard, east of Euclid Avenue.

Russell Froelich captured this stunning view (originally in color) of the theater district on Grand Avenue in 1944. America was in the midst of World War II, and people sometimes needed to get away from all the sacrifice of daily life, at least for a little while. The St. Louis was showing a Roy Rogers double feature.

This night view of a brightly lit St. Louis Movie Theater, at 718 North Grand Avenue, with the Missouri and American marquees in the distance, was taken in 1954. After years of the Great Depression and war, it was a good year to be out and about in the city and living the American Dream.

In the 1950s, this was the view looking north in the Grand Avenue theater district from the southwest corner of Lindell Boulevard and Grand Avenue. Once the western boundary of the city, the area had become an upscale neighborhood of fine homes and theaters by the late 1800s. The Fox, Missouri, American, Grand Central, and St. Louis theaters were all located along Grand Avenue. Today, the area is known as the Grand Center Arts District.

Around 1925, this lively group of partygoers have decked themselves out in their finest apparel and are ready to go out and light up the town—at a theater, nightclub, or party. There is a reason the era came to be known as the Roaring Twenties.

Thirteen people gathered for a celebration in front of the Old Rock House on the corner of Wharf and Chestnut Streets. The photographer and date are unknown, perhaps the 1930s, after the historic landmark had become a popular tavern and music venue. It was later dismantled and never restored as a historical site.

This spiffy drumming group livened things up on the back of a truck carrying a banner that reads, "All Together All The Time Makes It Easy To Keep St. Louis Clean." They drove around town, entertaining people and spreading the word about litter, pausing for this memorable portrait on Market Street in 1912.

This unidentified jazz band really knew how to ham it up, as evidenced in this promotional photograph by Block Brothers Studio about 1925. One source identifies the group as the St. Louis Cotton Club Band. Whatever their name, if they played as well as they looked, they must have been one great jazz band.

W.C. Handy is pictured on the album cover of *St. Louis Town 1927–1932*. The album featured recordings from several notable musicians, including Handy. He played the blues in the city in the late 1920s through early 1930s, when St. Louis became known for its unique style of music.

W.C. Handy visited the Old Rock House Saloon around 1935 for a reunion of sorts. Seen with other entertainers, Handy is seated with a cane. Admiring guests have gathered around the man who had already become a legend. Handy was a great musician, and his work remains popular among musicians today.

Lafayette Dancing Academy
GAZZETTE

Announcing

THE SNAPPIEST JAZZIEST COLORED ORCHESTRA

AL. MITCHELL

And His 7 High Class Entertainers

AT THE
LAFAYETTE DANCING ACADEMY
1800 SOUTH 18TH STREET

EVERY TUESDAY AND THURSDAY NITE

TICKETS
Ladies 20c - At Door - Gents 40c
Checking Gratis

Hall Rented For All Occasions

BELLEFONTAINE AND TOWER GROVE CARS DIRECT

The cover of this four-page circular for the Lafayette Dancing Academy, at 1800 South Eighteenth Street, announced that Al Mitchell and his orchestra were performing at the academy on Tuesday and Thursday nights. Admission was 20¢ for women and 40¢ for men.

BOOST

THE CARDINALS

AND

The Marigold Gardens

DELMAR AT HAMILTON
WE'VE WON THE

PENNANT

Now For The World

CHAMPIONSHIP

C'mon You Cardinals We're For You

FANS FROM ALL OVER

C'OUT AND DANCE TO THE DANCIEST DANCE
MUSIC YOU EVER DANCED TO.
ENTERTAINMENT EVERY NITE
Dancing 7 P M to One O'clock

Famous Marigold Gardens Orchestra

Manager   Make Reservations
J. C. CUSUMANO   CABANY 1320—2830—1390—5862

This deep-red card advertised a dance to promote the St. Louis Cardinals at the Marigold Gardens and featured the Marigold Gardens Orchestra. The event was held after the Cardinals had won the National League pennant and before the World Series, probably between 1926 and 1934. Fans were encouraged to "C'out and dance to the danciest dance music you ever danced to."

This somber photograph was taken at the old courthouse on June 20, 1930. A note on the back reads, "Scene of the last trial at Old Court House, Broadway & Market Sts. Division No. 6— Judge M. Hartmann, Presided; Adolph E. Zimmer, Clerk; Harry T. Stanton, Reporter & Henry Moehle, Deputy Sheriff . . . John C. Hobz, defendant, on witness stand, Mrs. Ruth Hobz, co-defendant sitting beside her attorney."

These men are past 60 and lost their jobs in the Depression. Neither expected to ever have a steady job again when John Vachon took this photograph in 1938. The men hopped freight trains from Omaha to Kansas City, to St. Louis, and back again. They picked up odd jobs and meals from a charitable person or a soup kitchen. (Courtesy of the Library of Congress, Prints & Photographs Division.)

Crowds of poor people joined the unemployed march along Pine Street during the Great Depression. In this 1931 photograph by Ralph A. Ross, the marchers demand, "We Want Jobs," and ask, "Where Shall We Sleep This Winter?" Both black and white marchers also called for an end to Jim Crow segregation and racial discrimination.

A mother and her son, along with several other women, linger on the sidewalk on the 5500 block of Delmar Boulevard about 1930. Several girls and older women enter and exit a shop. It appears that the boy has his eye on caramelized popcorn, cashews, and nuts, but money was tight, especially during the early years of the Depression.

In March 1936, when this photograph was taken, these crude shelters were referred to as a slum or squatter shacks. More accurately, it was a shantytown where unemployed men and women tried to make a home for their children with scraps of wood and sheet metal. (Courtesy of the Library of Congress, Prints & Photographs Division.)

This row of mailboxes was for squatters who lived in shacks along the Mississippi River in St. Louis in January 1939. It is hard to imagine getting through the winter in those unheated shacks of scrap wood. (Courtesy of the Library of Congress, Prints & Photographs Division.)

In 1938, this Greyhound station was about halfway between Memphis and St. Louis. If they could afford the fare, people boarded the bus to visit relatives or seek work elsewhere. They hoped that they might have better luck in other locales during the Great Depression. (Courtesy of the Library of Congress, Prints & Photographs Division.)

A driver stops to pay to cross the toll bridge over the Mississippi River while the attendant steps out of his booth on a misty day in January 1939. The country, was still in the dreary depths of the Great Depression. (Courtesy of the Library of Congress, Prints & Photographs Division.)

Young couples dance to live band music on the excursion boat *Admiral* about 1942. Despite the big band and crowd on the dance floor, there is a somber note on their faces. The men will soon return to action, and the women will go back to work in offices and factories that supply war materials to the men.

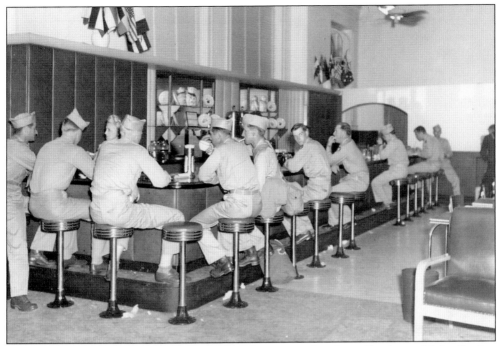

Soldiers hunker over the counter, occupying nearly every stool in the coffee shop at Union Station in this photograph by W.C. Persons. It is 1943 and the soldiers are either on a short furlough or, more likely, about to be deployed overseas. Some will never come home.

At Union Station, a helpful employee gives directions at the entrance to the shed in 1943. No other information is available about this photograph by W.C. Persons. It is likely the young woman has come to the station to meet a special soldier who is either coming home on a short leave or going off to war.

This photograph of travelers, including sailors, lined up at the ticket counter at Union Station was taken in 1945. A young soldier stands back from the others. It is the end of the war, and he appears uncertain about where to go from here and reluctant to purchase a ticket.

Taken in January 1939, this touching photograph by Arthur Rothstein captures a quiet moment in the life of one passenger. Sitting alone on one of the benches in the train station, she is reading what appears to be a letter. One can only imagine what news she has received. (Courtesy of the Library of Congress, Prints & Photographs Division.)

Six

OUT AND ABOUT IN FAIR WEATHER

A young woman skates tentatively over the ice on a lake, probably in Forest Park. Photographed by Carl Michel around 1915, she appears to be a little anxious about the possibility of falling in this risky venture. But she also seems to delight in the experience of gliding over the ice.

A woman pulls a child through the snow on a sled at a city park, probably Forest Park, and they are having great fun. All of the high speed, including the boy's separation from the sled and impending tumble, was captured in this amusing photograph by Carl Michel about 1915.

A large crowd has braved the cold to come out and enjoy a winter afternoon of ice skating on the lake at Carondelet Park. In this photograph, taken by W.C. Persons around 1935, the skaters have spread all over the lake. Everyone seems happy to be outside and skating away.

It may have been a frigid winter day, but the sun has come out, and people are having fun skating on a frozen pond in Forest Park. It is January 1947, and the trees are bare, and the ground is covered in a blanket of snow. But all the skaters—men, women, and children—are smiling and laughing.

Young men and women take a break from skating to huddle around a bonfire at Forest Park to warm up their hands and feet. It is January 1, 1947, and bitterly cold. However, the war was over, and the young people appear to be ringing in a pretty good New Year.

Three generations of the Gladfelter family gathered for this picnic on a warm summer day in the 1880s. Everyone from little children to grandparents is represented in the group portrait—along with an array of hearty dishes spread out on the blanket in front of them.

Taken in 1897, this photograph by Emil Boehl shows that drifting along in a rowboat can be quite relaxing after working a long day at the office or tending to the children at home. Better yet, boating on Forest Park Lake is an ideal way of impressing, and hopefully romancing, that special girl—even if she insists on rowing the boat.

Around 1900, this group relaxes at a summer picnic in a city park with baseball and beer. The men are drinking the beer, while the girls pose in front with bat and glove in hand. They are the only picnickers ready to play ball.

This is how gentlemen fished in 1895—in suit and tie often topped with a derby hat. There was no need to venture into the heart of the wilderness. At their leisure on a pleasant afternoon, sitting comfortably on a park bench, this throng of men and boys try their luck fishing from the bank of a pond in Carondelet Park.

A boy and a woman, probably his mother, enjoy a tranquil moment together at the edge of the water. They are watching the boy's model sailboat drift under a bridge in a city lake, most likely at Forest Park, around 1910. What better way is there to spend a quiet evening in the summer?

A man in a straw boater fires the starting gun, and they are off—eight women in a hobble-skirt race. These races became popular about 1910. The intense action was captured by Charles Trefts around 1912. Interest in this type of competition had faded by 1915.

Held in 1914, the Pageant and Masque attracted more than 75,000 people and 7,500 local volunteers. The theatrical extravaganza commemorated the 150th anniversary of St. Louis and 300 years of local history. People spread over the slope of Art Hill in Forest Park, picnicked, soaked up the sun, and had a thoroughly wonderful time in anticipation of that evening's five-hour, two-part performance: a pageant that told an allegorical tale through dance and pantomime.

Decked out in the latest fashions of the day, probably in the mid-1920s, these two young women are getting outside to see and be seen in their stylish dresses, shoes, and hats. The photographer and location are unknown. After a long winter, however, the ladies certainly want to bask in the afternoon sun of a spring day.

These boys are enjoying the competition at a fishing derby in Fairgrounds Park in 1948. Apparently, the fish were biting under the arch of the bridge that day, and everyone has rushed there to go after them. So much for having a secret fishing spot.

THE VELOCIPEDE MANIA—WHAT IT MAY COME TO!—[Drawn by Thomas Worth.]

The caption screams, "The Velocipede Mania—What it May Come To!" in this illustration from *Harper's Weekly* of May 1, 1869. Drawn by Thomas Worth, the artwork portrays people riding their bicycles along a crowded street. Some are pulling carts, and others have goods strapped to their backs. A vacant horse stable stands next to a horse meat market, with a velocipede manufactory and riding school next door.

On the Fourth of July in 1892, these young people pose with their bicycles in Forest Park. The girls are wearing white blouses with black skirts, and the boys are in white shirts and black pants. Names on the back are: "Miss Marrion Dunials, Mr. Leo Bathol, Miss Louise Anderson, Mr. A.J. Howard, and Miss Maud Dunning—later Mrs. John de Smet Hurck."

A young man and woman ride their bicycles side-by-side down a gravel road in the countryside, perhaps on their way to Musick's Ferry. The road is rough, but they seem comfortable together. It is a clear Fourth of July in 1892, and riding bikes was a pleasant way to enjoy the holiday.

In "Taming the Bicycle," Mark Twain wrote, "Get a bicycle. You will not regret it. If you live." Here, in 1895, a group of men have paused on their road trip in Pike County while one of them repairs his bicycle's chain. His friends seem patient, although no one is lending a hand. Clearly, it can be frustrating if one's bicycle breaks down in the country.

A man and woman on a tandem bike, or bicycle built for two, are pictured on a nature trail lined by thick bushes in 1897. The woman is wearing a long skirt, long-sleeved shirt, boots, and a hat. And the man has wisely chosen pants, sweater, boots, and a handkerchief tied around his neck.

These ladies and gentlemen have paused to rest on a porch during a "bicycle party" and left their bicycles strewn around them. The women are properly attired for a road trip in long-sleeved blouses, long skirts, boots, and hats. The men are decked out appropriately for 1897 in white shirts and hats. Smart riders are also wearing straw hats for a little shade.

With their heads popping out of the water like fishing bobbers, these two women and a man in the Lyon family are cooling off with a swim in a lake. The lake and photographer are unknown, but this moment in the bathers' lives was captured around 1905. Clearly, they are having a pleasant evening in refreshingly cool water.

The girls in this class not only learned to swim, but also entertained an audience of neighborhood residents at Mullanphy Pool, located at Eleventh Street between Cass Avenue and Mullanphy Street. However, the pool had sobering signs too, with injunctions against spitting in the water because of the threat of deadly tuberculosis.

During "women's swim time" in Mullanphy Pool at Eleventh Street, the girls and young ladies had the place to themselves. They are clearly having fun splashing around and cooling off on one scorcher of a day in the summer of 1914.

Seated on a riverbank, these swimmers at a Locust Club swimming party in 1921 paused for a moment to be photographed by Oscar Kuehn. One man in the group is wearing a jaunty Navy cap, and four women are wearing stylish swimming suits and caps that leave everything to the imagination.

Sunbathers have sprawled out on the sandy shore while swimmers take a dip and others paddle canoes at Lincoln Beach on the Meramec River. This photograph was taken in the 1930s, in the depths of the Great Depression, but everyone put their troubles aside, drove out to the river, and enjoyed a thoroughly pleasant day.

Four young women pose in bathing suits at a Curtiss-Wright evening swim party on August 25, 1943. No bikinis here, but the styles were risqué enough for the 1940s. Curtiss-Wright was a major aviation company and defense factory during World War II. These four worked in the offices or factory to supply fighting men with the weapons they needed to win the war.

Katie McCullough, standing at left in the rear, and Rose E. Taylor came to the Fairgrounds Park swimming pool with their lawyer George W. Draper II. The women were demanding entrance into the public pool from Supt. Louis Fierer on June 19, 1950. At the time, African Americans were denied admission to public pools, even on the hottest days of summer, because of their race.

After they were denied entrance to the public pool because of race on June 19, 1950, L.S. Curtis demanded in a strong, dignified manner that St. Louis recognize the civil rights of African Americans. He insisted that Supt. Louis Fierer must allow African Americans, including his sons, to swim at the Fairgrounds Park pool.

Pictured are members of the "famous world beaters St. Louis Browns" baseball team in 1888. The dashing players are wearing striped coats over their baseball uniforms. Team members include a young boy, the "Browns Mascot," seated in the back row and two dogs up front.

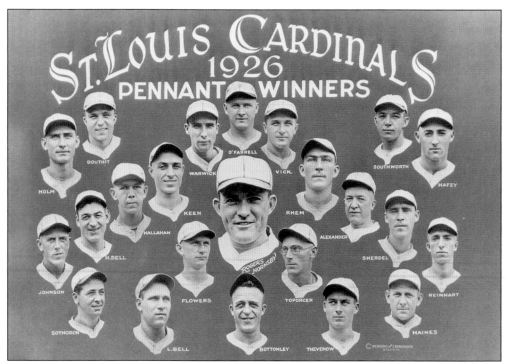

This team photograph includes a small portrait of each ballplayer on the great St. Louis Cardinals team of 1926. The name of each player is printed next to his portrait. Star hitter and infielder Rogers Hornsby is featured prominently at center.

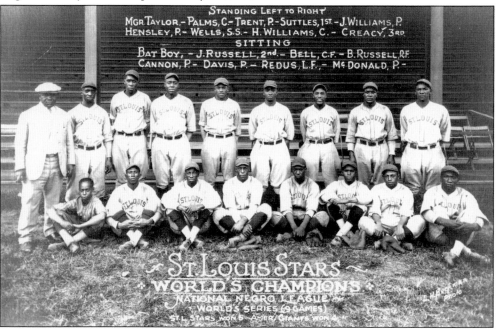

St. Louis has had its share of winners, including the St. Louis Stars. In 1928, the team posed for this portrait after they won the Negro League World Series against the American Giants. The players' names are listed above their portraits.

In this classic portrait, the Dean brothers Dizzy and Paul are sitting on either side of the legendary Babe Ruth. The Deans are dressed in their Cardinals uniforms, while Ruth is wearing a suit and hat and sporting a Cardinals pin. The three baseball stars appear to be posing under the stands.

Three legendary baseball stars came together for this photograph at the World Series. Shaking hands are, from left to right, George Sisler, Babe Ruth, and Ty Cobb. Cobb said that Sisler, first baseman for the Cardinals, who could play several different positions, was "the nearest thing to a perfect ballplayer" he had ever seen. (Courtesy of the Library of Congress, Prints & Photographs Division.)

The St. Louis Browns were the 1944 American League pennant winners. Members of this amazing team are seated in three rows in the stands at Sportsman's Park. The batboy is kneeling in front, and the coaches are standing on either side. Their names are written on the front of the photograph.

Taken by W.C. Persons in the 1930s, this photograph shows Cardinal fans seated in the stands at Sportsman's Park with their eyes fixed on the game. Coca-Cola and Pabst vendors are hard at work serving up ice-cold beverages to all the thirsty fans in each section of the stadium. One hopes that the Cardinals won that day.

A crowd of spectators in the stands at Sportsman's Park intently watch the game on Ladies' Day, as photographed by W.C. Persons in 1939. Teams played at Sportsman's Park, beloved by St. Louisans, from 1920 to 1966.

Stan Musial poses in uniform in the 1950s at Sportsman's Park with fans in the bleachers. He stands, bat in hand, as if ready to hit the next pitch. Musial, who epitomized the Gateway City, once said, "I have no hesitation to say that St. Louis is a great place in which to live and work."

About 1910, a store guard and policeman walking his beat posed together on the sidewalk outside the Globe department store at Seventh Street and Franklin Avenue. The officer is dressed in his official police uniform while the guard is sporting an impressive Globe uniform. Curious people look on behind them.

About 1935, Market Street between Seventeenth and Eighteenth Streets was a tough area of saloons and hotels known as the Bowery. Proprietors of these enterprises had colorful names such as Jimmy the Mule, Bantam Daly, and Bad Jack William. Police chief John J. McCarthy said that an ordinary citizen was lucky to get away from the street with the gold still in his teeth.

As he walked his beat in a rough part of town, this policeman posed with a woman and her child on a rickety balcony, most likely at the rear of the tenement where it would be out of sight. Taken in the 1940s, this photograph illustrates that the Great Depression might have ended, but not poverty.

An able fireman holds a team of sleek horses ready to be harnessed to the new fire wagon. They are standing in front of the fire station at Eleventh and Lucas Streets in the early 1900s. The St. Louis Fire Department relied completely on horses for transportation until 1910, when its first motor-driven apparatus was acquired.

Behind the steering wheel, this dignified firefighter is delighted to show off the brand-new Dorris IBW hose and chemical car of the St. Louis Fire Department. Made in St. Louis, this vehicle was the latest technology on wheels. The car was assigned to the Union No. 2 fire station in 1918.

The St. Louis Fire Department fire engine and crew pull out of Engine Company No. 24 ready for action in 1930. Two firefighters occupy the driver's seat of the shiny new truck, one behind the steering wheel, and several other men are standing on the back.

A group of street maintenance workers lined up at the edge of the sidewalk, and street cleaners, drawn by white horses, are parked against the sidewalk at North Tucker Boulevard and Market Street. The St. Louis Plating Co. and Russell's Dinner are in the background in this turn-of-the-20th-century photograph.

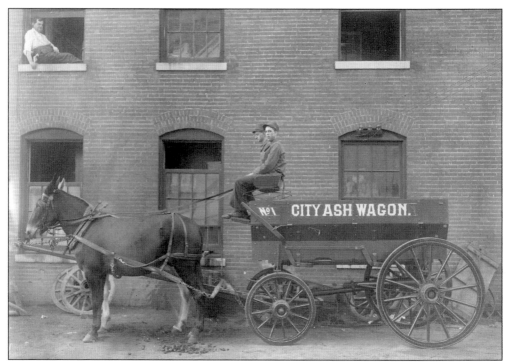

Ash collection from fireplaces, cast-iron stoves, and coal furnaces was once a necessary city service. Here, two workmen are perched on the bench of a wagon pulled by a pair of mules. The wagon reads: "City Ash Wagon No. 1." It was apparently the first of such vehicles in turn-of-the-century St. Louis. In the background, a man is sitting on the ledge of an open window.

A Mogul street-sprinkling truck is parked on an unidentified street in 1913, probably to show off the latest technology. Patented by F.A. Stiers, the truck certainly looks as if it could sprinkle plenty of water to wet the dust down. It must have been especially useful on hot, dry days of summer.

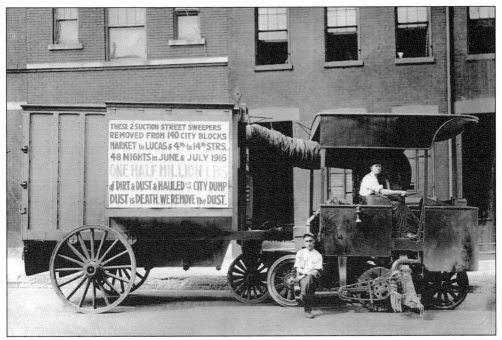

Two city workers casually pose with their state-of-the-art street sweeper in 1916 on an unidentified street in St. Louis. City officials have slapped signs on the sides of the vehicle that boast of its efficiency along with a public service notice that warned citizens about the dangers of dust.

City workers are upgrading the ground between streetcar tracks on an unidentified street. The photograph was probably taken around 1935. Piles of bricks line each side of the track. One worker sweeps debris, others prepare the track, and a skilled man lays bricks, one after another.

In 1959, a young lady in her Sunday best and an older woman look over the merchandise in the toys and games department at Stix, Baer & Fuller. This department appears to be well stocked with Hula-Hoops. The popular store was on the northeast corner of Seventh Street and Washington Avenue.

It is lunchtime for these busy shoppers at the Stix, Baer & Fuller diner on August 2, 1961, and time for a break from browsing merchandise. Judging from the large number of ladies occupying nearly every stool at every counter, the food must have been as good as the shopping.

Pope's Cafeteria at 3538 Washington Avenue had an inviting front in 1953. The name of the restaurant is prominently displayed above the entrance and exit. A menu is posted by the front door. A rooftop sign at left advertises hams, bacon, and sausage. The interior of the restaurant, including people at tables, can be glimpsed through the window.

Taken on July 1, 1953, this photograph of Pope's Cafeteria shows the pillars, tables, chairs, and the serving line at the end of the lunch rush. Workers stand behind the serving lines while others have cleared tables and are now washing stacks of dishes. A group of latecomers are enjoying a quiet lunch at this classic cafeteria.

Louis DeHatre stands behind the counter of his diner, Louie's Place, a landmark at St. Louis Municipal Flying Field (Lambert Field). Slices of pie are laid out on serving plates on the top shelf. Food is kept warm on the steam tables below, and behind Louie is a counter with plates, a warming oven, and canned goods.

This Dixie Diner, home of the "Dixie Sandwich System," was on the northeast corner of Sixth and Pine Streets. It was a good location with many pedestrians. These diners featured the 5¢ Dixie hamburger and other lunch specials, like 10¢ bottle beer, 10¢ ham and eggs, and 5¢ Coneys. Customers were to be extended "courtesy and service."

The spotless interior of the Dixie Hamburger Stand, located at the corner of Watson Road and Chippewa Street, was furnished with chrome stools and the classic countertop of a diner in 1941. Wedges of homemade pies line the back edge of the counter. The diner is polished, even shiny, and ready to take orders from hungry customers.

This classic diner, complete with chrome stools running along the counter, was a local hangout in the 1930s and 1940s that invited passersby to "Have a Hoffie." With catchy names like "cakewich" and "bunwich," their sandwiches were advertised as a "Snack in a Sack," "No Slip," and "No Drip" in this photograph taken about 1942.

This photograph captures a moment in the life of the Parkmoor, possibly at Big Bend and Clayton Roads near Washington University. This is how the local landmarks looked around 1935—and for several more decades. If any diner had become a favorite with St. Louisans, as well as visitors to the city, it was the Parkmoor.

A waitress efficiently serves up food and soda pop orders to the after-school crowd at the Parkmoor at 324 DeBaliviere Avenue. When this photograph was taken in the 1950s, Freddy Spriggs was the manager, and the diner was a real hot spot for young high schoolers to get together after a long day in the classroom.

This promotional brochure for Parkmoor restaurants features an image of a carhop on the job, and another of a young woman skillfully demonstrating the latest technology and innovations of 1960. The carhop could now immediately call in orders from the customer's car door to the kitchen for some really "fast food."

An energetic carhop cheerfully hustles a tray with a customer's order to their parked car at a Parkmoor restaurant about 1960. Over the decades, all Parkmoor restaurants in St. Louis retained their character and flavor as classic diners with great food and cheerful carhops, waitresses, and counter clerks.

Catherine Boehl and her friends did not have to travel far to get together in 1880. When they wanted to step out and have a cup of coffee, they donned their finest apparel and sauntered over to Boehl's backyard. The ladies sat formally in this group portrait. Even as they were slipping into the past, they were content with their own time and place.

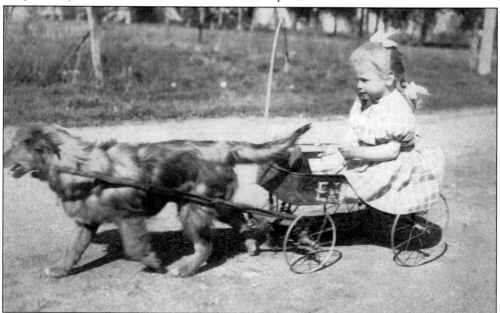

Around 1910, a young girl is thrilled to be riding in a wagon pulled by her dog in this action shot by William Trefts. It appears that she is learning from an early age how to get out and about town, or around her own neighborhood at least. With her determined face, it is obvious that she is going places, and everyone better get out of her way. For some reason, the term "hell on wheels" comes to mind.

Well, this is one way to get out and about in the city. Photographed by W.C. Persons about 1925, these women are posing with an elephant named Miss Jim at the St. Louis Zoo. The ladies are cool, calm, and amused, as if they were simply taking the lovable pachyderm out for a stroll around Forest Park. Miss Jim also seems to delight in all the attention.

DISCOVER THOUSANDS OF LOCAL HISTORY BOOKS
FEATURING MILLIONS OF VINTAGE IMAGES

Arcadia Publishing, the leading local history publisher in the United States, is committed to making history accessible and meaningful through publishing books that celebrate and preserve the heritage of America's people and places.

Find more books like this at
www.arcadiapublishing.com

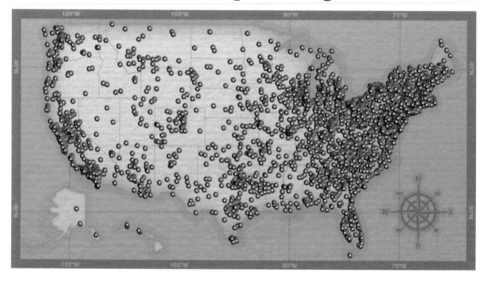

Search for your hometown history, your old stomping grounds, and even your favorite sports team.

Consistent with our mission to preserve history on a local level, this book was printed in South Carolina on American-made paper and manufactured entirely in the United States. Products carrying the accredited Forest Stewardship Council (FSC) label are printed on 100 percent FSC-certified paper.

MADE IN THE